Loving Jesus, Transforming Lives

Experiencing and Imparting the Extravagant Love of God

Michael Carter

sermontobook
.com

Sermon To Book
www.sermontobook.com

Loving Jesus, Transforming Lives / Michael Carter
ISBN-13: 978-1-945793-55-4
ISBN-10: 1-945793-55-4

Every person is called of God to fulfill a specific purpose. There are no substitutions or replacements. God has given His purpose to everyone. However; there is one theme in the Bible that everyone is ultimately and equally accountable for in their lives. This purpose is God's love fulfilled in the heart of those who follow after Him. In his book *Loving Jesus, Transforming Lives*, Pastor Michael Carter provides an in-depth and thoughtful study of the perfect will of God. This book will help new believers grow in Christ and challenge those seasoned in the faith. It is with great honor and privilege that I highly recommend this book. Read it with the expectation of being transformed into a faithful servant of the King of kings and Lord of lords.

—Pastor Patrick Bucksot, Associate Pastor of Breath of God International Outreach Church, in New Bern, NC

Loving Jesus, Transforming Lives is more than a book about God's great love toward us and our reciprocal love in return. It is a well of inspiration, an instruction manual, and a practical tour guide all rolled up into one significant volume. With profound simplicity, scriptural insights, and the use of practical illustrations, Pastor Mike addresses the all-important truth of coming to know God's extravagant and transforming love through Jesus Christ. Pastor Mike further demonstrates that our transformation by such love was then meant to lead us into a divine commission—a commission to become channels of God's extravagant love to everyone, everywhere. By including review questions at the end of each chapter, it becomes an excellent tool for the purpose of discipleship and group study. Thanks, Pastor Mike, for this most excellent work!

—Pastor Philip Cappuccio

In his book *Loving Jesus, Transforming Lives*, Pastor Michael Carter has put forth the essence of personal transformation, experiencing and releasing the love of Jesus. In the most practical terms, lessons of love [...] are shared that if released in and through your life, will bring significant impact to your life and the lives of others. Knowing Michael, I am confident this book was not developed clinically through the sterile environment of study alone but was born out of a life lived "out loud," in the real world where we all live and serve. Michael has served his Savior and us all well through this effort.

—Pastor David Frech, Senior Pastor, Church of the Harvest, Olathe, Kansas

Pastor Michael Carter offers the reader a wonderful and complete insight into the vastness of God's love toward us, the extravagance of that love, and the purpose behind that love. This work is most obviously delivered from the heart of a loving pastor to his congregation, and now we've been given the opportunity to receive from that heart as well. I would encourage you to purchase this book, incorporate it into your life, and let the truths expressed here so simply and graciously be expressed from your own heart and ministry.

—Dr. Jerry David, Pastor Emeritus of Lincoln City Church, Lincoln, Nebraska

I dedicate this book to my late grandmother, Jesse Ruth Stringer, who sacrificed her life daily for her family and forced me to memorize Philippians 4:13 as a child.

To my pastor and spiritual father, Philip Amandola, who taught me integrity and godly wisdom. You are truly an inspiration and surely have transformed my life.

CONTENTS

Receiving and Giving Love 3

Imitating God's Love...5

Discovering the Love of God...25

The Power of Shared Love 45

The Four "One Anothers"...63

Transformation...77

The Extravagant Love of God...97

Notes 99

About the Author 100

About Sermon To Book...102

Receiving and Giving Love

Most of us know we are called to love other people—but did you know that God wants more from you than that? He has called you to love other people, to walk in love every single day, *the way that Jesus loves them* (Mark 12:29–31). That doesn't mean that some days you will love people and other days you won't. That doesn't mean that you love people only when you feel like it. That means you are to love other people with God's kind of love—the love that Jesus Himself has shown you.

But how can you know how to love other people, if you haven't first experienced God's love for you? Until you first understand and see what Christ has done for you, you will never be able to put it into practice in your life, to love other people in such a way that will transform both your life and theirs. God shows His love for us through His Son's actions: Christ poured Himself out as an offering, a sacrifice. He gave His very life for each of us (Romans 5:8). When we really grasp what He has done for us, when we experience it for ourselves, we learn from Him how to walk it out in our own lives and in our relationships with other people. And that is where true transformation in our relationships can begin.

Are you looking for more in your walk with God and in your relationships with other people? Are you seeking more love—more passion—in your life? Then keep reading! Loving Jesus is the key to loving other people, loving yourself—and changing your life.

CHAPTER ONE

Imitating God's Love

Therefore be imitators of God, as dear children. And walk in love, as Christ also has loved us and given Himself for us, an offering and a sacrifice to God for a sweet-smelling aroma.

—Ephesians 5:1–2

The Love of the Father

Have you ever heard your own words come out of your child's mouth? To imitate someone means to copy what he or she does. Watch what God does and then do it—that is what it means to be an imitator of God. Just as children watch their parents and then copy what their mom or dad does or says, we too learn our ways of speaking and being, from our heavenly Father.

Mostly what God does is to love His creation. That's what He does. Many people think God is just like their earthly fathers, maybe unavailable, or perhaps harsh or unloving or hard to please. Our Father does chastise us and correct us, but His primary motivation for everything that He does is a deep, abiding, unconditional love. And when He tells us to keep company with Him, He is asking us to learn a life of love from Him.

God's love is not cautious—it's extravagant (1 John 3:1)! He gives in abundance, with abandon, to His children. He didn't choose to love us to get something from us, but to give everything of Himself to us. And we are to love like that, too. Does that seem like an impossible task? At first it may seem impossible, especially if you really think about it. If it doesn't seem impossible to you, then you may not be *really* thinking about just how much God is asking from you.

When I was in prayer about this very matter, this is what the Lord shared with me: *If you can understand the love that I have for you, how I have given everything of Myself to you, then obedience to Me won't be a problem for you.* And it is true! If you truly grasp everything that God has done for you, how much He really loves you, then you will have no problem at all doing what He asks you to do. You will watch the words that come out of your mouth. You will be kind to other people. You will have a good attitude. You will listen to what other people say to you. And it will come naturally to you.

All these things are possible when we follow God's example of how to love. Consider how God has asked you to love:

Love suffers long and is kind; love does not envy; love does not parade itself, is not puffed up; does not behave rudely, does not seek its own, is not provoked, thinks no evil; does not rejoice in iniquity, but rejoices in the truth; bears all things, believes all things, hopes all things, endures all

things. Love never fails.
                    —1 Corinthians 13:4–8

Verse 13 of the same chapter tells us that in addition to all of this, only three things will remain: "And now abide faith, hope, love, these three; but the greatest of these is love" (1 Corinthians 13:13).

Each of these three things is necessary: We must have *faith* in God and trust steadfastly in His promises to us. And we must have *hope*, unswerving and unwavering. But the thing that holds all of this together is to *love* extravagantly!

Pray this prayer with me right now:

> Lord Jesus, today I ask that You help me to understand and accept Your love. Help me to have the eyes to see and the heart to respond to the needs of others. Let me share grace with the undeserving and bring healing to the hurting. I want to love extravagantly the way that You do. In Your name I pray, amen.

I don't know about you, but that's what I want. I want to be able to share grace and bring healing to hurting people around me. If you have never tried this before, I've got to tell you that one of the greatest feelings in the world is to help share the real answer to life's problems—Jesus Christ—with someone who is in need. The desperate people of the world need what we have. So many people are desperate for an answer, but to give the love of Jesus to them, you need to live a certain way. You live with Him in mind, knowing that you are His representative wherever you go.

When you don't have the love of Jesus inside of you, you will also live a certain way—whether you want to or not, whether you recognize it or not. When you don't have the love of our Lord, you are unfortunately living without the rule of love in your life. Your relationships will suffer; your children will suffer; the *world* will suffer!

First John 4:8 says, "He who does not love does not know God, for God is love." A person who does not know love does not know God. Why? Because God is love. God doesn't just love—as an action. No, it's who He *is*. Without this kind of love living on the inside of you, you will be limited in how you can respond to the people around you in your life.

A Life Without Love

Have you ever noticed that most people do not listen in a conversation with the intent to understand? Most people in a conversation listen with the intent to reply. You may have noticed that with other people, but have you ever noticed that about yourself? Ask yourself if you are truly listening to others to really hear them or if you are distracted by your own chatter in your head.

This is just one of many examples of how we as human beings choose to live a life without love—often without even realizing it. If we don't allow God's love to permeate our lives, will we ever be able to *really* love someone else? If we believe that God is love, wouldn't it stand to reason that there is no love without God?

What have you previously believed is the definition of

"love"? Maybe you have thought it was compassion, caring, empathy, or even generosity. But those things are the *result* of what love does, not love itself. Love itself produces these things; and without love—God's love—in your life, those things will be sadly missing, affecting not only you, but everyone around you.

Living a life without Jesus means living a life without love—because God is love. If you choose to live that way, you will find yourself becoming hardhearted, unsympathetic, even cold at times. You will be insensitive—maybe without even knowing it. You will be unkind, heartless, unfeeling, without compassion. And this will begin to affect your relationships. You will become indifferent and find yourself not caring about the people around you or the world in which you live.

Have you caught yourself thinking, *Well, I really don't care? I don't care who becomes president. I don't care who my boss is. I don't care what time I get to work. I don't care who the speaker is this week at church. I don't care about this, and I don't care about that.* If you begin to live so indifferently, that lack of sensitivity will soon become ingrained within your spirit and affect the entire world around you.

If you live that way, you will lose your passion. You will become isolated and begin to live your life alone, not involved in anyone else around you. But not caring about anyone else's problems or concerns is not an option when you love like Jesus. You will become involved when you love like Jesus. You have to care—you can't help it! And how many people in this world simply need someone to listen to them? So many people would love for someone to listen to their concerns. Maybe you don't have every single solution to what they are experiencing, but you do have two things they need: a listening ear and a compassionate heart.

Many years ago, someone placed an ad in a newspaper that read: "I will listen to you talk for thirty minutes without comment, five bucks."[1] The person who placed the ad promised to listen for half an hour without comment, without judgment, without negativity. It might have sounded like a hoax, but the person was serious. It wasn't long before this individual was overwhelmed by the number of phone calls. The pain of loneliness was so great for many people that they were willing to try anything. Even answer a newspaper ad and pay a stranger for half an hour of companionship. They needed someone to listen to them, even for just thirty minutes, and they were willing to pay money to make that happen.

If you are a person who loves like Jesus, you are the answer to the prayers of so many people all around you. You don't necessarily have to have all the answers. You may not know even one answer. But you *can* listen, and you *can* love. If you don't have Jesus, you will live a life of self-pity, always feeling sorry for yourself, but if you do have Jesus, you will not be focused on yourself. You will be offering your very self, your heart, your compassion, and your love to the world.

A Life of Self-Pity

I myself used to live a life of self-pity. If you are living that way, I hate to step on your toes—but self-pity is, by its definition, a very selfish perspective to take. People who are overcome with self-pity are always looking for sympathy from others. Everything in the world is something "owed" to them. And when things don't go their way, well, then, life is completely unfair. They are always down on themselves; they are always comparing themselves to others—and always coming up short. The other person has nicer things, a better job, a better car.

Or how about this? The other person is more involved in church. They know more scripture passages or seem closer to God. No matter what it is, people engrossed in self-pity are always comparing themselves to others.

There is a great danger in comparing yourself to other people. When you begin to do it too much, you will *always* find that *everyone else* is better than you. You will be drawn further and further into the self-pity trap, which always leads to negativity. If you want to live a negative life, if you want to experience only negative attitudes, feelings, assumptions, and opinions, then follow the path of self-pity.

So many people have negative assumptions about their future because something negative happened in the past—and if you look closely at that attitude, it too is based in self-pity. Break that cycle! If you have already made up your mind about what's going to happen tomorrow because you were disappointed yesterday, understand that *God is not like that.* You don't have to feel sorry for yourself because of what has already happened. Look forward to the wonderful things that are yet ahead!

Some people think they are an island. If you live like that, you will be living without the love of Jesus. You will be living in isolation. You will avoid people. When you see someone who might need something from you, you turn and go the other way, or you cross the street. When the phone rings, you don't answer it, thinking, *it could be somebody who needs something from me.*

Once an old man was on a crowded bus when a younger man got on the bus and took the seat next to him. The younger man asked the older one, "What time is it?" The old man didn't answer. The younger man tried again: "Excuse me, sir. What time is it?" The old man again said nothing. He just turned and looked the other way. The young man moved to another seat on the bus and eventually got off at the next stop.

The man in the seat behind the old man couldn't keep quiet. He leaned forward and asked, "Why were you so rude to that young man? He only asked you for the time."

The old man replied, "Well, yeah, but if I had given him the time of day, then he would have wanted to know where I am going. Then we might have started talking about our interests, and if we had done that, he might have invited himself over to my house for dinner. If he came to my house, then he would meet my lovely daughter, and if he met her, they would both certainly fall in love. And, frankly, I don't want my daughter marrying someone who doesn't have a watch."

The old man was so closed off to the idea of a new relationship and where it might lead that he was willing to go to great lengths to avoid it.

A person engrossed in self-pity thinks to themselves, *I don't want to be anything to anyone. I don't want talk to anyone. I just want to be by myself.* I don't know if you have ever been that way, but I'll confess something to you: there have been many times in my life when I've been that way. If someone wanted to talk to me, I would immediately start to complain in my mind: *What do they want to talk about? They will start talking to me, then we will probably talk more, and then we will probably become friends. That's going to take up my time. I'm over here doing nothing, but they will be interrupting me from my doing nothing!*

I once read a story about a woman who, being thoroughly disgusted with her husband, not only wanted to divorce him but also wanted to hurt him as much as she felt he'd hurt her.

One day she went into her minister's office, full of hatred, and vented her feelings to him. She explained that she and her husband constantly argued and her husband never said, "I love you." This woman was so upset that she wondered aloud why she'd married him in the first place. She explained that she felt as though she'd wasted the best years of her life in an unfruitful marriage.

The minister listed to the woman's' story and immediately came up with an imaginative plan whereby the woman could exact her revenge. He told her that if she really wanted vengeance, she must first go home to her husband and treat him as if he were the love of her life. She should act toward him and speak to him, the minister suggested, with all of the affection and consideration she wished he would show toward her.

Of course, the woman was hesitant, but the minister persuaded her that convincing her husband of how much she loved him—and *then* ambushing him with a divorce—

was the best way to get back at him.

Now determined to carry out the minister's evil-genius plan, she spent two months being exceptionally kind to her husband. She spared no compliment and showed him an abundance of love and patience. She listened to him with understanding and spoke to him with the utmost respect.

Then, after the two months, the woman went back to the minster. He asked her if she was ready to shock her husband with a divorce.

But the woman was bewildered. She told the minister she wouldn't dream of divorcing her husband anymore! After so many weeks going out of her way to act like she loved her husband, she finally remembered how much she really did love him.[2]

Her actions had actually changed her feelings. Her motion resulted in emotion. Her ability to love was established, not so much by a fervent promise as by her repeated deeds. The point of this story is not that she changed his love toward her, which might possibly have happened as well; the point is that she changed her love toward him.

Some people need to act more like Jesus so that their hearts will then become more like Jesus' heart. You can choose to live in a way that is hardhearted and indifferent, isolated, negative, and filled with self-pity, or you can live your life filled with the love of Jesus. Choose to live your life the "Jesus way."

A Full Life

Jesus said that He was "the door," that if anyone would enter heaven through Him, they would be saved and have eternal life (John 10:7–9). Jesus told us that He came so that we could have life. His purpose is very different from the purpose of our enemy. Satan, our adversary, came to kill us, to steal from us, and to destroy us, but Jesus came so that we would have an abundant life (John 10:10).

When we live the "Jesus way," our lives are filled with possibility, and our thoughts change to become filled with positivity. If we are asked, "Do you think you can do that?" our answer becomes, "I don't know, but it's possible! We will see. I will pray and see what the Lord has to say about it. If it's not in God's will, it will not happen—something better will—but other than that, it is possible!"

When we begin to live our lives with expectancy, our attitude will change, and we will understand that with God all things really are possible. Jesus said that all things are possible to the person who *believes* (Mark 9:23).

I would say to you what the prophet Samuel told Israel in the days of the Old Testament, "Now therefore stand and see this great thing which the LORD will do before your eyes..." (1 Samuel 12:16). He was not saying, "Well, let's see whether or not the Lord does it, and if He does, then we will applaud." No, he said, "Stand up and look with expectancy at what God is about to do. Open your eyes to what God is doing and what He will do."

That's how you live your life when you have the love of Jesus operating in your heart. You have a "full tank" from which you can give freely: a tank full of virtue, full of life, full of dreams, full of love, full of energy—full of *God*. Your heart contains all that you need, all that you want, everything that you live for.

It is important that you understand what the love of Christ is so that you can go out and share it with everyone around you. That is the purpose of living life "on full." When you live life as if it is full of possibilities, you are living a life that is strong in the Lord. You are strong in grace and in resources. You don't shrink back from situations, circumstances, or other people. When they ask you for the time of day, you give it to them, knowing that they might talk to you a little longer. You can defeat the enemy, overcome any situation, and influence those around you to thrive in the same way. We were made to achieve the goal and provide the same kind of strength for other people around us.

As a young man, my favorite time of year was always March Madness—basketball season. Even my daughter asks me during the month of March, "How is your bracket?" I'm not alone; lots of people really get into it. One of the reasons is the excitement that is generated toward the end of the season. It's not like it is during the middle of the season, when if you lose a game it's okay, because you can just get back up and try again on Thursday. No, toward the end of the season, if you lose today, that is it for the rest of this season. The players play each game as if there is no tomorrow.

Coming down to the last moments of a game, a game that you cannot lose, the suspense builds. Have you ever heard the saying that when you go into something, you should not "play to lose"? If you are playing to lose, you are being too safe, too cautious. If the game is tied 68 to 68, you might not want to turn the ball over. You might want to be sure you have a good shot, and if you don't, then you might just back out of it. The team that decides to play that way loses every single time. The team that takes chances, that is aggressive, that sticks to the game plan and is all in is the team that will win the game—and likely the entire tournament.

In the game of life, the only way for us to be successful is to be all in. You cannot live your life on the sidelines, shrinking back and thinking, *Oh, I will just let her do it. Or, I'm not going to try. I could go to school, but I don't want to because I might fail. I don't know if I'm smart enough. Or, I will just keep this job. I won't try to look for another. I might make my situation worse.* You cannot live that way and expect to have a strong life.

God wants us to be strong. In the New Testament, Timothy was admonished to "be strong in the grace that is in Christ Jesus" (2 Timothy 2:1), and God says the same thing to you and me today. We are to be strong and stand in grace. Philippians 4:13 tells us that we can do all things through Christ who strengthens us. If we live with strength, we will also begin to live with purpose. Purpose is greater than potential when it comes to achieving what God has set forth for you to do.

What is your purpose? What is the reason that you have been placed on this earth? God has put you here for a reason, and He wants you to fulfill that purpose, not simply rely on your potential. Potential is what you *might* be able to do. Potential is a hope. If you think that maybe you can do a certain thing, then you have the potential to do it.

But God goes further than that. He has placed a purpose upon you, and there is no "hope" about it. There is no question about it. You *can* fulfill your purpose. A life filled with purpose is a life that sees the target. A life that is lived intentionally is a life in which you say, "I'm going for it. I will not back down. I will not shrink back. It is all about my purpose!"

You are not an accident. You have been fearfully and wonderfully made (Psalm 139:14). There are many plans in each man's heart, but the Lord's counsel is what will stand (Proverbs 19:21). Man's plans are established by wise counsel, but it is God's plans that will ultimately stand (Proverbs 20:18). Because you are not an accident, you can know that God has specific plans in mind for your life! And His love for you provides the impetus you need to discover those plans—and to live them out.

> *Now to Him who is able to [carry out His purpose and] do superabundantly more than all that we dare ask or think [infinitely beyond our greatest prayers, hopes, or dreams], according to His power that is at work within us...*
> *—Ephesians 3:20 (AMP)*

Think about that verse for a minute: God's love for you is what crafted His purpose for you from the very beginning. He loved you when He first thought of you and conceived of His plans for your life. The actions of His power are now at work within you to carry out that very purpose for your life—to change the world far more than you could even ever imagine!

Consider your highest prayers, desires, thoughts, hopes, and dreams—and then try to imagine infinitely beyond that. God is able to do all of this and more. He has said, "But indeed for this purpose I have raised you up, that I may show My power *in* you, and that My name may be declared in all the earth" (Exodus 9:16–17). But how is He able to do this? It is through you and me.

In conclusion, living a life of love means choosing to focus on being a conduit for the life and love of Jesus, flowing out to other people. Jesus came to transform lives with His love. You are meant to be used by Jesus, to be like Jesus, to share like Jesus, and to love like Jesus. Your eyes are to be the birthplace of kindness.

You can't care until you are aware, so slow down and look around. Stop and talk with people. Begin to see people like Jesus sees them. Don't wait. Do what you can in every moment, starting today. Now is the time to live like Jesus and to share His love.

If you don't understand the love that He has for you, then I dare you to take the chance to discover His love. It will require something from you. You may need to be vulnerable to a point. You will have to open up and listen to what the Lord says. But the reward—fully experiencing God's love, sharing it with other people, and changing the world by fulfilling His purpose for your life—is beyond compare!

Chapter One Questions

Question: Why is understanding God's love crucial to truly loving others?

_____

_____

_____

_____

_____

_____

_____

_____

_____

_____

Question: Concerning what areas or people do you find yourself saying "I don't care"? Is your indifference simply prioritizing your time and energy or is it indicative of a lack of love? How can you tell the difference?

_____

_____

_____

_____

_____

_____

_____

_____

_____

Question: Is your life most characterized by self-pity, potential, or purpose? How can you move toward a life of purpose and positivity?

_____

_____

_____

_____

_____

_____

_____

_____

_____

_____

_____

_____

Action: List the ways God's love has been extravagant in your life. How can you share that extravagance with the people who come across your path? Choose to step outside your "comfort zone" and speak or listen to a stranger this week. Ask how you can pray for your new acquaintance, and if possible, follow up with them a few days later.

_____

_____

_____

_____

_____

_____

_____

_____

_____

_____

Chapter One Notes

_____

_____

_____

_____

_____

_____

_____

_____

_____

_____

_____

_____

_____

_____

_____

_____

_____

_____

_____

_____

CHAPTER TWO

Discovering the Love of God

For I am persuaded that neither death nor life, nor angels nor principalities nor powers, nor things present, nor height nor depth, nor any other created thing, shall be able to separate us from the [prevailing] love of God which is in Christ Jesus our Lord.

—Romans 8:38

God's love is so far above our human love that it can be mind-blowing to think about!

Have you ever really thought about what Romans 8:38 means? Human love can change, based on emotions, circumstances, or what another person has to offer to our own self-centered needs. But God's love never, ever changes: Nothing separates us from it! It is prevailing over anything that might oppose it: It is a love that proves itself to be more powerful than any opposing force, a love that is not only victorious, but also widespread. God's love is all of these things.

You may have heard Romans 8:38 repeated many

times, but really let it sink in: *Nothing* can separate you from God's love. His love prevails, no matter what comes against it. No matter what twists and turns in life come your way, His love will always cover you, because it always prevails. His love is greater than anything that could ever happen to you.

Human love is different. It usually extends from our emotions. For instance, maybe I look at my wife and I can see that she's so beautiful. Her beauty sparks an emotion inside of me, and I hear myself saying the words "'I love you." My love for my wife stems from many other things, but God's love stems simply from Him, just because He loves. None of us did anything to cause Him to love us. He just does.

When a new mother delivers her baby, she looks at the child that she holds in her arms, and before the baby ever has an opportunity to say, "'Mom, I love you," or, "Mom, can I do something for you?" or anything else, that mother loves her baby. In a similar way, God's love for us is unconditional.

God loved you before He even created you. You were created because of His love. His love for you is so deep-seated within Himself that He actually used that love to create you.

That's what the phrase "fearfully and wonderfully made" (Psalm 139:14) means: there was a love in play already, before you came into being. God didn't spot you across a crowded room and say, "Wow, yes, I love you." No, He loved you *and then* He saw you. That kind of knowledge ought to give you the assurance that there's truly nothing that can separate you from the love of our

Lord.

God's definition of love would boil down to this: the "giving of oneself at the expense of oneself for the benefit of others."

A Life of Love

The Word tells us: "For God so loved the world that He gave..." (John 3:16). God the Father willingly and freely gave His only begotten Son to save us. Romans 5:8 declares, "But God demonstrates His own love towards us, in that while we were still sinners, Christ died for us."

Jesus died for us in faith. He died on the cross before any of us ever accepted His free gift. He didn't wait for us to make a declaration of faith. No, while we were still wallowing in our sins, still in the miry clay of improper thoughts and impure deeds, filthy communication and ungodly behavior, even then Christ was on the cross, dying to redeem you and me from ourselves.

Isn't God's love extravagant? There is no love like the love that God has for you. He gave Himself, completely and wholly. Jesus left His heavenly home to come and wrap Himself in human flesh, ultimately to lay His life down for us, and because of this we can know love.

Not only is God's love extravagant to our human minds, but it goes beyond human understanding in another way: God's love never holds a grudge. As 2 Corinthians 5:19 tells us, "God was in Christ reconciling the world to Himself, not imputing their trespasses to them...." This passage simply means that God does not bring up your sins to make you feel bad or hold things over your head.

He has reconciled with us and now recognizes us as His dear children.

Jesus demonstrated this type of love when He walked on the earth—and He showed us what our heavenly Father is like. Jesus never held a grudge; He had compassion that far exceeds our own human understanding.

In what is my favorite Bible story, a woman was brought before Him. She had been caught red-handed in the act of adultery, and her accusers threw her down before Him (John 8:3–4). According to the Law, the punishment for her sin was death by stoning, but the accusers wanted to trick Jesus, so they asked, "What do you say?" (John 8:5) Then the greatest force this universe has ever known spoke. *Love* spoke, and He said, "You who have no sin should cast the first stone" (John 8:7)

Every single accuser left, from the youngest to the oldest. That would have been great if that was the end of the story.

But here is my favorite part of my favorite story: When they had all left the scene, Jesus Himself bent down before this woman, and in today's terms, He said, "Sweetheart, where are your accusers? Who accuses you of this sin?" Her reply was, "There are none, Lord." His final statement? "Neither do I. The greatest force in the universe—My love—does not accuse you. So, go and sin no more" (John 8:10–11).

Good Gifts

And finally, one of the most wonderful ways in which God loves His children is by giving us good gifts.

Matthew 7:11 points out that if we "being evil, know how to give good gifts to [our] children, how much more will [our] Father who is in heaven give good things to those who ask Him!"

The Word also tells us, "Every good gift and every perfect gift is from above, and comes down from the Father of lights, with whom there is no variation or shadow of turning" (James 1:17).

What kinds of good gifts have you received from your heavenly Father? A good job? A loving family? A solid roof over your head? What about a healthy body? Food on the table? Or other intangible things like love, joy, and peace in your life? All the gifts God gives to you are proof that He loves you as His own precious child!

In addition, one of God's greatest gifts is described in 2 Corinthians 1:4, which tells us that God "comforts us in all our troubles, so that we can comfort those in any trouble with the comfort we ourselves receive from God" (NIV). Did you know that there is a reason that God comforts you? It is so that you might be able to comfort others.

God is near you now, and He desires to help you. God is coming into your world to meet your needs. Jesus reaches out for those who stand afar off, those who are embarrassed, those who are totally on empty, and those who cannot reach out to Him with their own power. Jesus comes to where we are. That is what God's love is like.

Showing God's Love to Others

Most of us likely struggle with the idea of God's

unconditional love at times, because some people truly do seem unlovable. If we are realistic about it, many of us would have to admit that we have some family members who come across as flat-out unlovable. And if you can't think of any family members or friends who are unlovable, then just look in the mirror!

The love you have been given from God is not just meant for you; it's also for others. In Isaiah 55:8–9, God told Israel through His prophet Isaiah, "'For my thoughts are not your thoughts, neither are your ways my ways,' declares the LORD. 'As the heavens are higher than the earth, so are my ways higher than your ways and my thoughts than your thoughts'" (NIV)

Consider those verses in another version: "'I don't think the way you think. The way you work isn't the way I work.' God's Decree. 'For as the sky soars high above earth, so the way I work surpasses the way you work, and the way I think is beyond the way you think'" (NIV). God's ways are so much different from ours!

The Lord then went on to say this: "As the rain and the snow come down from heaven, and do not return to it without watering the earth and making it bud and flourish, so that it yields seed for the sower and bread for the eater, so is my word that goes out from my mouth: It will not return to me empty, but will accomplish what I desire and achieve the purpose for which I sent it" (Isaiah 55:10–11 NIV).

God's Word will always accomplish what He has set out for it to do! God's love is just like His Word. He sends it forth to accomplish a purpose, and that's what it does. His love doesn't come back to Him unless or until it has accomplished what it was sent out to do. In other words, He loves us, and in turn we go forth to love others. In this way, His love becomes a prevailing kind of love. His love will always win!

God's Love Helps Us to Love Others

Did you know that God always expects something back when He sends things out? When He sends out His love—and He has sent His love out from Himself and given it to you—He will be rewarded. He takes joy in seeing His love spread throughout the earth. He is rewarded when the love that He shows to you and to me is in turn expressed to His other children throughout the world.

That may be hard for us to see or understand at times, but His love will prevail. His grace and His mercy will always win out in the long run.

The love of God is stronger than we ever dare to hope or dream. It's stronger than any sin we could ever commit. No matter what you may have done, His love is far above it, because His love prevails. It can be so difficult for us to understand God's love, but we cannot talk about loving others until we truly understand what love is, what God's love is, and how it prevails in our lives. David Sanford wrote:

> Here is what love is like ... genuine love. God's kind of love. It's patient. It can wait. It helps others, even if they never find out who assisted them. Love doesn't look for greener pastures. Love doesn't boast. It doesn't try to build itself up to be something it isn't. Love doesn't act in a loose, immoral way. It doesn't seek to take, but it

willingly gives. Love doesn't lose its temper. It doesn't keep changing its mind. Love doesn't think about how difficult the other person is, and certainly doesn't think of how it could get back at someone. Love is grieved deeply over the evil in this world, but it rejoices over truth. Love comes and sits with you when you're feeling down and finds out what is wrong. It empathizes with you and believes in you. Love knows you'll come through just as God planned, and love carries on to the end. It doesn't give up, quit, diminish, or go home. Love perseveres, even when everything goes wrong and the feelings leave and the other person doesn't seem as special anymore. Love succeeds 100 percent of the time. That, my friend, is what genuine love is.[3]

When we have experienced God's love, we can then love others the way He asks us to. God's love never fails; it prevails!

If you understand how great God's love really is, then what should you do with that? How should you ultimately respond? You will find yourself beginning to love the people around you *unconditionally*, without hesitation and without expecting the same in return, without disappointment at not receiving the same in return— because we are receiving what we really need from God Himself.

When we don't understand God's love, we may become disappointed in the circumstances in which we find ourselves. Chances are that at some point you have had these thoughts: *Things didn't work out the way I thought they would. Why would God bring me to this place and open this door for me, only to close it in my face? I don't understand that, and I'm disappointed.*

Our disappointment often stems from us not having a

full comprehension of God's love. We can become disillusioned if someone appears to be less than what we originally thought they were, if a job that we take isn't as good as we thought it would be, and so on. Disillusionment brings disappointment. Some of us get disillusioned with God: *I thought He was all-powerful. I thought He loved me. I thought His love never failed, but look at the war and the sin and the famine in the world. Look at the children dying!*

Disappointment in God can lead to anger with God. Have you ever gotten mad at God? It's okay to say that you have. I will admit it myself. I love the Father, and I know that He loves me, but if things don't work out the way I want them to, I still tend to become angry. I ask God, *Why did You let this happen? This is not the way it's supposed to be!*

This kind of disappointment and disillusionment actually stems from a lack of understanding God's love and how it overcomes any obstacles in its way. We become discouraged or a little weary. We keep trying and keep running our heads into a wall. We keep running our shoulders into a door and not getting anywhere. But at these times, God would say to you, "Don't give up! My way of loving will bring great reward to your life!"

And let us not grow weary while doing good, for in due season we shall reap if we do not lose heart.
—Galatians 6:9

If we allow disappointment to lead to anger and anger to lead to resentment, we can become bitter and callous.

We might build walls around our hearts to try to protect ourselves. We may say to ourselves, *I'm never letting anyone else in ever again. I'm not going to wear my heart on my sleeve anymore. I'm not going to put myself out there. I'm not going to interview for any more jobs. I'm not going to audition for any more parts. I'm not going to do anything new. I'm tired of failing.*

Some of us have made the inner vow: *I'm never going to tell anyone I love them ever again. I'm not going to do that! I'm just going to live my life, then die and go to heaven.* We all want to go to heaven, but we certainly get tired of being hurt along the way. The temptation is to close ourselves off from other people and keep to ourselves, but this attitude stems from a lack of understanding of God's prevailing love.

God will absolutely wreck your plans when He knows that your plans will wreck you. God can see this coming. Because He loves you, He will come in without hesitation to change your life. He will tear down your plans, tear them completely apart, when He knows that their destruction is the best thing for you. We may see destruction wreaking havoc in our lives. Suddenly our lives are laid to waste before us.

We need to understand that some things have to be broken before God can shape them the way He wants them to be. If we try to shape our lives ourselves, they would still be imperfect, but if we allow God to mold our hearts and minds, our experiences, and our relationships, then we can trust that they are part of His perfect will and His perfect plan.

We make plans to do one thing, but God already has

plans for something else. Don't become discouraged when it seems like things aren't working out in your life. Keep faith that God loves you and will fulfill His purpose for you. Don't get stuck in how you thought things should be. Instead, look at what God is doing now and stay positive!

How Does Perfect Love Behave?

God's love prompted Him to send His Son to earth to die on the cross for our salvation. The familiar Bible verse John 3:16 says, "For God so loved the world that He gave His only begotten Son, that whoever believes in Him should not perish but have everlasting life."

Note that this verse *doesn't* say that God so loved the world that He *saved* the world; it says that God so loved the world that He sent His Son to sacrifice Himself, to give His life in a gruesome and horrifying death on the cross. God the Father didn't just snap His fingers and say, "Oh, well, they messed up. I'll just go ahead and save the world." He had to pay the price for our salvation with His perfect blood.

First John 4:10 tells us, "In this is love, not that we loved God, but that He loved us and sent His Son to be the propitiation for our sins." Paul told the Corinthians that "you are bought at a price…" (1 Corinthians 6:20). Jesus' work on the cross fully satisfied the demand for our death. That's how much He loves you—He sacrificed Himself to save you. And not just you, but the whole world: "God so loved the world…" (John 3:16) His love includes everyone, no matter where they are or what they have done. There is nowhere on this earth or anywhere else in the universe where God's love cannot reach us. It is all-encompassing.

God's love is also eternal; it doesn't end. God's love is not hot for us one day and cold for us another day. He doesn't treat us the way that we treat Him. Instead He shows us what true love, His kind of love, entails. The psalmist said twenty-six times in Psalm 136 that "His mercy endures forever." Jeremiah also wrote, "The LORD has appeared of old to me, saying: 'Yes, I have loved you with an everlasting love; therefore with lovingkindness I have drawn you'" (Jeremiah 31:3).

It is not that we loved Him, but that He loved us. With lovingkindness He drew us to Him, and His love doesn't stop. God will never stop loving you! God's love is eternal, and His love is perfect. And as the Bible tells us, perfect love casts out all fear (1 John 4:18). God's perfect love removes our fear, enabling us and empowering us to pass that same love on to the people He has placed in our lives.

Again, God's love is so perfect that it can't even make sense to us. This perfect love is not about getting what we deserve, it's not about being right in our own eyes, and it's not about looking out for ourselves. No, it's all about others. Perfect love is the opposite of self-centered "love"; it's the opposite of being self-absorbed and self-seeking. Perfect love is all about sacrifice. It's all about the other person.

Eating at Grandfather's Table

There's a popular tale, originating in the Southwest, of an elderly man who had to go live with his son, his son's wife, and his young grandson. The old man was very weak and in need of care. When he sat at the table to eat with the family, he would spill his food on the table and on the floor. He sometimes even dropped his utensils and dishes.

Finally, the old man's son and daughter-in-law got fed up with his messes and his broken dishes. They set a small table in the corner where he could eat out of a wooden bowl. The child noticed how this saddened his grandfather, who was left feeling alone and unwanted, but his mother and father remained harsh and unrelenting.

That is, until the day the father noticed his son sitting on the floor and fashioning something out of wooden scraps. When asked what he was doing, the child replied that he was making a wooden bowl for his parents to eat out of when they grew older and it was his turn to take care of them.

Suddenly ashamed, the boy's parents brought their elderly father back to the family table to share their meals— and from then on, when he dropped some food or a dish, they responded with graciousness and compassionate instead of cruelty.[4]

As hard as it is for us to grasp, we have to understand that this is the kind of love God has for us. No matter how many times you spill your milk, no matter how many times your peas roll off your spoon, no matter how many times you drop your food on the floor, God still says you can eat at the table. You can eat at the Master's table because His love has made it possible!

His Personal Love

In addition to all these other things, God's love is personal. God loves the world, God loves His Church, and God loves people. But you also need to understand that God loves *you*. In Genesis 2, God saw that the man He had made, Adam, was alone, and He knew that the only way to fill the void of loneliness was to extract from him what God had put in him for companionship (Genesis 2:18–24). God's love is personal. He didn't bring a lion or an elephant or a tree or anything else to Adam. He crafted the perfect companion, Eve, for him, because He knew Adam and He deeply understood his personal needs.

God loves you in the very same way. He knows you— inside and out. He comforts you, strengthens you, heals you, and brings purpose and meaning to your life. He showers you with His good gifts, and then empowers you to take that love out into your relationships you have with the people in your life. What an amazing gift God's love really is!

In Luke 8:48, Jesus leaned down to the woman with an issue of blood and addressed her as "daughter." He didn't just say, "Hey, lady, you are healed, and now I've got other stuff to do!" No, He said, "*Daughter,* be of good cheer; your faith has made you well. Go in peace." In other words, He was telling her to have comfort, to have no more worry and no more fear. He was confirming that He had set His love upon her so that now, wherever she went, she could go in peace.

LOVING JESUS, TRANSFORMING LIVES · 39

Jesus said similar words to the woman caught in adultery. "Where are your accusers?" was His question. "There are none, Lord," she answered. Jesus' response? "Neither do I accuse you" (John 8:10–11).

The Ruler of the universe, the One who created you, says to you, "I breathed the breath of life into you (Genesis 2:7). You are fearfully and wonderfully made (Psalm 139:14). I placed you on the potter's wheel (Jeremiah 18:6). I have the power to give your life and the power to destroy you. I can wrap the universe up in a scroll and throw it away. When I breathe, stars come out of my mouth (Psalm 33:6 NIV). But I don't accuse you! You are free, so go in peace."

The Bible says that whenever Jesus saw the multitudes of people, He was "moved" (Matthew 9:36). The God of the universe was moved with compassion for them because they were hungry, both physically and spiritually. When you understand how moved He is by the needs of His people, you will also understand how He longs to meet your own needs—every single one of them—but also use you as a conduit of His power and blessing to meet the needs of the world around you.

That means that God has a plan for your life! Isaiah 49:16 also tells us these words of our Lord: "See, I have inscribed you on the palms of *My hands*." Your name is right there, written on His hand. He takes it everywhere He goes. He never forgets or overlooks you. He sees you. He knows you more deeply than you know yourself. He loves you with an everlasting, indestructible, unconditional love (Jeremiah 31:3).

God has numbered the very hairs on your head

(Matthew 10:30). He has put all your tears in a bottle (Psalm 56:8). He loves you that much, and He is moved with compassion by your needs. His prevailing love toward you is personal. What more could you ever need? You don't need to look for love in any other place. What more do you need to foster more love in your life? Learn how to share that love with other people.

WORKBOOK

Chapter Two Questions

Question: How is God's love different from human love? In what ways can human love help us understand a little of God's love? How would you describe unconditional love?

_____

_____

_____

_____

_____

_____

_____

_____

_____

_____

Question: Have you ever been disappointed or angry with God? When was a time that you doubted His love? What was faulty in your perspective or in your understanding of what His love means?

_____

_____

_____

_____

_____

_____

_____

_____

_____

_____

Question: What do Jesus' life and death reveal to us about God's love?

_____

_____

_____

_____

_____

_____

_____

_____

_____

_____

_____

_____

Action: God's love for you is personal. Choose three passages about God's love. Write them out with your name in them (e.g. "The Lord has loved [insert your name] with an everlasting love."—from Jeremiah 31:3).

_____

_____

_____

_____

_____

_____

_____

_____

_____

_____

_____

Chapter Two Notes

CHAPTER THREE

The Power of Shared Love

Watch what God does, and then you do it, like children who learn proper behavior from their parents. Mostly what God does is love you. Keep company with him and learn a life of love. Observe how Christ loved us. His love was not cautious but extravagant. He didn't love in order to get something from us but to give everything of himself to us. Love like that.

Ephesians 5:1–2 *(MSG)*

When we learn to walk in love, it becomes a sacrifice, a sweet-smelling aroma to our Lord (Philippians 4:18). We become like Him. His love is not cautious; it is extravagant! Jesus didn't hold anything back in His love for us, but He gave everything that He had. He didn't love us to get something from us, but to give everything of Himself to us. And He calls us to love other people in the very same way.

First Corinthians 16:14 tells us: "Let all that you do be done in love" (ESV). Another translation says it this way: "Let love prevail in your life, words, and actions" (VOICE).

Let love prevail. Do you remember that word from the last chapter? *Prevail.* When love prevails in our lives, it becomes our primary motivation, the impetus behind everything that we do.

Touch the Hem of His Garment

A very sick woman once came up to Jesus, fighting her way through a crowd (Mark 5:27). Jesus had been walking with His disciples, and a great crowd had gathered around Him. He was on His way to perform a miracle for someone else, but the crowd was all around Him, "thronging" around Him (Mark 5:31). What that means is that they were groping and grasping for Him. His disciples were walking beside Him, likely pushing hands away, trying to keep people at an arm's distance so that the Rabbi, the Master, could continue His journey to where He would work His next miracle. Until this little woman arrived on the scene.

Matthew 23:5 NLT, referring to the Pharisees, tells us that "on their arms they wear extra wide prayer boxes with Scripture verses inside." The Gospels indicate that Jesus wore tassels on the four corners of His outer robe (Matthew 9:20; 14:36; Mark 6:56; Luke 8:44). Although there is no explicit evidence in the Gospels, He also may have worn phylacteries. If that were the case, it is understandable why this woman might try to touch Jesus' garment—because the Word was there.

She may have seen one of the Pharisees walking by and recognized the words of God on his garment. But then she would have looked over and seen the throngs of people and the disciples who had become apostles. In the middle of all that, something caught her eye. It was the *Word of God*—the living, breathing Word of God made flesh (John 1:14)—and I believe that right then she realized something.

She realized that the letter of the law kills, but the Spirit gives life, and the Word of God was there in the flesh to bring her that life (2 Corinthians 3:6). She wanted to touch the hem of the living Word of God's garment. She didn't want some dead scripture; she wanted the living, breathing Word. So, she crawled on, making her way through the throngs of people. This woman who had an issue of blood finally reached out and clung to the hem of His garment. Immediately Jesus turned and asked, "Who touched Me?" (Luke 8:45). He knew that someone had touched His robe and that healing power had left Him.

Peter probably had a bit of a smart mouth in this situation. I know. I probably would have been just like him. "Hey, Jesus," I would probably have said. "You're supposed to be the Master here. You've got a lot of insight. Has anybody touched You?" Peter said: "Master, the multitudes throng and press You" (Luke 8:45). In other words, of course someone had touched Him! The crowds of people were pressing in all around Him. But Jesus explained, "Somebody touched Me, for I perceived power going out from Me" (Luke 8:46). In other words: "What I'm saying is that a small amount of virtue left Me just then. Some power left My body." The point is that Jesus had virtue and power inside of Him. You cannot give something away that you don't first already have.

If we don't go to Jesus and press in close to Him, if we

don't discover God's love for us, if we don't understand that His love prevails and that it's the greatest force in the universe, then we will never have this kind of love available to give to other people. We'll just be giving them our feelings and our emotions. We might even be giving them our lust.

In other words, we give to other people what's within us to give. If you don't have the love of Jesus in you, you cannot give it. Pray with me right now:

> Lord Jesus, today I ask for a double portion of the love of God. Fill me to overflowing and help me to have eyes to see and a heart to respond to the needs of all the people whom I encounter each day. Lord, let me share Your grace with the undeserving and bring healing to the hurting.

As you pray, "let me share Your grace with the undeserving," take a good look at yourself—because *you* are the undeserving. We all are the undeserving. And when you pray the words, "bring healing to the hurting," understand that this is the very reason that Jesus came. He came to bring healing to the hurting. And He asks that you do the same, to the ones He brings across your path.

The Good Samaritan

Luke 10:25–37 tells the story of the Good Samaritan, which was a response to a question posed by a lawyer who wanted to trip Jesus up.

The lawyer asked Jesus what he needed to do to gain

eternal life. Jesus asked him what *he* thought, and this man—an expert in the Mosaic law—replied that it was, first, to love God, and second, to love one's neighbor as oneself (verse 25–27).

But the lawyer wanted to justify himself, so he asked Jesus, "And who is my neighbor?" (verse 27). Jesus answered his question with a story (verses 30–34):

> *A certain man went down from Jerusalem to Jericho, and fell among thieves, who stripped him of his clothing, wounded him, and departed, leaving him half dead. Now by chance a certain priest came down that road. And when he saw him, he passed by on the other side. Likewise a Levite, when he arrived at the place, came and looked, and passed by on the other side. But a certain Samaritan, as he journeyed, came where he was. And when he saw him, he had compassion. So he went to him and bandaged his wounds, pouring on oil and wine; and he set him on his own animal, brought him to an inn, and took care of him.*

The good Samaritan didn't stop there: on the next day, when he departed, he gave the innkeeper two denarii and said, "Take care of him; and whatever more you spend, when I come again, I will repay you" (verse 35).

Jesus then asked the lawyer, "So which of these three do you think was neighbor to him who fell among the thieves?" (verse 36).

The answer to Jesus' pointed question is given quite directly in the Scriptures: "He who showed mercy on him." Then Jesus gave the final moral of the story: "Go and do likewise" (verse 37).

In other words, we are being asked to find out how God loves us, what He does and how He does it, and then we are to go and do likewise. We need to learn what love like that is really all about, and then we need to share it with other people.

There are six points I'd like to discuss with you out of the story of the Good Samaritan. As familiar as some of us may be with this story, it can still be difficult for us to understand how to put it into practice in our lives.

First, *shared love does not pass by a need.* The priest and the Levite passed on the other side. These were people who could have helped, but they chose not to do so. These types of passersby dole out compassion based on perceived worth. They think, *I will feel sorry for you if I feel that you're worth it, but if I don't feel that way, then hey, you really just need to get it together.*

The priest and the Levite were coming down the road from Jerusalem. They had already performed their religious duties. They had already prayed. They had already helped the number of people they felt they needed to help that day. You may feel this way, too, sometimes. You may have already called someone on the phone and encouraged them. You may have already prayed for someone. You may feel that you have done your Christian duty for the day.

The priest was a man of the Word, likely someone who performed sacrifices in the Temple. He might have been a person who had the privilege of going deeper in the Temple than anyone else could ever go. He may have pressed in to the literal presence of God in the Holy of Holies—but when it came to helping his neighbor, he failed miserably! The two passersby in Jesus' story were religious, but they were caught up in a lifeless religion.

Their attitude was, *I can see your need, but I won't do anything about it.*

Shared love does not pass by the need. Shared love gets up in the morning and says, "How can I help someone today?"

Second, *shared love starts with you,* even if you feel like the most unlikely person. You may not feel that you can love someone with godly love. You may not feel that you have it together enough to be of any real help to anyone. Have you ever had these thoughts? Maybe you don't think you're educated enough or wealthy enough. Maybe you don't think you have enough Scripture memorized to give the right answer if someone asks you about being a Christian. Or maybe, like Moses, you don't think you have the gift of gab to talk easily to other people.

And yet, you are the unlikely person God has put into place to share His love. Did you realize that the Samaritan was actually the most unlikely person to be a "neighbor" to the man on the side of the road? He was technically the most unqualified of the three examples in Jesus' story. The Samaritans in Jesus' day were half Jewish and half Gentile. They were thus rejected by both groups, ostracized by religious and secular cultures and communities.

In other words, this man didn't walk around with Scripture boxes on his garment, and he wasn't coming from the Temple where he had just entered the Holy of Holies. He hadn't come from giving a great sermon or laying hands on the sick and healing them. No, he was just walking down the street when he saw a need and decided to do something about it.

The Samaritan could have ignored the wounded Jew and left him to die or even finished him off, since Jews and Samaritans hated each other. He easily could have convinced himself that he wasn't qualified to help or that it wasn't his responsibility. After all, if the situation were reversed, would a Jew really help him? But the Samaritan didn't do that. He simply saw someone in need and chose to do what he could to help. He chose to love.

You may feel like an unlikely candidate to help the people around you, but you may be the very person whom God has chosen for the job. You probably don't have it all together, and you may not feel prepared, but God is calling you to do what you know to do.

Third, *shared love starts where people are,* and it starts right where you are. The Bible tells us that the Samaritan "came to where he was." The Levite and the priest both passed by on the other side of the road, but the Samaritan came over to where the hurting man was to help.

The Samaritan had likely gone through some hard times himself. Maybe he had been beaten and robbed in the past. Maybe he could relate to the man on the side of the road. Maybe someone had helped him in the past, and he knew how much it meant. Or maybe he hadn't received help when he needed it, and he knew what that felt like.

Whatever the case, the Samaritan saw the man who was in need, and he moved himself in the man's direction. To help people you must move towards them, where they are, and start from that point. It will take a concentrated effort, and it's usually not convenient. If it were convenient, then everyone would do it.

Fourth, *shared love starts with seeing and being moved*

LOVING JESUS, TRANSFORMING LIVES · 53

by the need. You can't be hard-hearted or self-absorbed and be a person who shares the love of God. You have to see the need and be moved by the need. Matthew 9:36 says of the Lord Jesus: "But when he saw the multitude he was moved with compassion for them..."

Fifth, *shared love starts with doing something about what you see.* It is never enough just to have compassion or empathy. It's never enough just to feel sorry for someone else. James 2:15 states, "If a brother or sister is naked and destitute of daily food, and one of you says to them, 'Depart in peace, be warmed and filled,' but you do not give them the things which are needed for the body, what *does* it profit?"

If you see someone in need and all you contribute to the situation is to say, "That's rough. That's a tough break. I wish things were different in your life," what good does that really do? Sharing love means doing something about what you see.

Luke 10:34 tells us: "So he went to him and bandaged his wounds." The Samaritan did what it took to help. He poured out his own oil and wine. He put the wounded man on the back of his own animal and took him to the inn. He spent the night at the inn and took care of him. The Samaritan did something about what he saw. Through his actions, he shared love.

Finally, *shared love costs something.* The next day, when the Samaritan saw that the wounded man wasn't yet ready to go, he went the extra mile by giving the innkeeper additional funds. He said, "Take care of him; and whatever more you spend, when I come again, I will repay you" (Luke 10: 35). He was willing to spend whatever it took to ensure that the man received the care he needed.

This is going the extra mile in life, and it comes from following Jesus closely. Our Lord said that if a man asks you to go one mile with him, we are to go the extra mile (Matthew 5:41). This is the love that Jesus lived by. And He didn't just show it occasionally; Jesus lived His entire life by this love.

This may not be the most popular message in the world. Many people prefer to hear the message out of Deuteronomy 28 that tells us we are blessed in the city and blessed in the field, that we are blessed when we come and blessed when we go out, that we are the head and not the tail—and all of that is true (Deuteronomy 28:3–6, 13). But there is a reason we have been blessed: to be a blessing to other people.

Second Corinthians 1:4 tells us: "[He] who comforts us in all our tribulation, that we may be able to comfort those who are in any trouble, with the comfort with which we ourselves are comforted by God." The Samaritan was offering the comfort of the heavenly Father. He caught the concept that the same thing we receive from God we must then turn around and give to other people. This is the essence of what the world needs: Find out how God loves and love like that. See what God does and then go and do likewise!

If we don't share God's love, everything He has given us is for nothing. If we don't share the abundance that God has given us, then what are we accepting it for? Are we saying outwardly that we are unselfish, but really, in our hearts, we are selfish? Do we say that we are others-focused, but really, in our hearts, we find that we are self-centered? If that is the case, others will be able to see it. As Jesus said, a tree is known by its fruit. We can look at an apple tree and immediately tell that it's an apple tree. If it's got apples on its limbs, it's an apple tree.

It is the same way with our hearts. John wrote in the New Testament: "But whoever has this world's goods, and sees his brother in need, and shuts up his heart from him, how does the love of God abide in him? My little children, let us not love in word or in tongue, but in deed and in truth" (1 John 3:17–18). James, another disciple of Jesus, said, "I will show you my faith by my works" (James 2:18). You can talk the talk all day long—it may start in your mind, grow in your heart, and finally be confessed out of your mouth—but there must be *action* with your faith or it's just hot air!

Jesus was the greatest example of someone who shared love. In fact, Jesus shared everything that was in Him with us. He already shared it with you when He went to the cross. Jesus had everything when He was in heaven. He created the heavens and the earth. He had all the power in the world, but because you and I were lost, He wrapped Himself in human flesh and shared His love. It cost Him everything. It cost Him pain and anguish. It cost His very life. Now we are called to receive that love and give it away to a hurting world.

We must have the love of Jesus in us before we can share it. If you find yourself dealing with these points and you aren't sure whether you can walk them out in your own life, keep praying to ask the Lord to help you. Press into the presence of the Lord; get into your prayer closet.

God will expose everything in your heart to you, but

don't be afraid of it. Don't hide from the Lord. He will expose to you the things that need to be exposed, and then He will fill you with His unconditional, unending love, the greatest force in the universe. He will till the ground of your heart and make it a place of good soil and fertile ground where God can plant His seeds of love to share with the world.

WORKBOOK

Chapter Three Questions

Question: Why did the sick woman want to touch Jesus' garment? How did she put Jesus' love on display that day? Can others look at your life and see the power of Christ's love transforming you?

_____

_____

_____

_____

_____

_____

_____

_____

_____

_____

Question: In what practical ways did the Samaritan show love to the injured man? Why was he a surprising hero in this story, especially compared to the two who passed by? Have you ever been surprised by receiving love from a stranger or enemy? Which person in the story best typifies the way you respond to others' interruptions, needs, and crises?

_____

_____

_____

_____

_____

_____

_____

_____

_____

_____

_____

Question: Why is it so important to share Jesus' love? What does our ability to share Christ's love, or our lack of sharing, reveal about our relationship with Him?

_____

_____

_____

_____

_____

_____

_____

_____

_____

_____

_____

Action: The Samaritan took action, even costly action. List five community needs, names of hurting people, or tough situations around you. Next to each, write a specific action that could help (note that there is a difference between love *costing* something and throwing money at a problem so that you don't have to get personally involved). Then choose one specific action plan you will start on today.

_____

_____

_____

_____

_____

_____

_____

_____

_____

_____

_____

_____

_____

Chapter Three Notes

_____

_____

_____

_____

_____

_____

_____

_____

_____

_____

_____

_____

_____

_____

_____

_____

_____

_____

_____

CHAPTER FOUR

The Four "One Anothers"

Behold, how good and how pleasant it is for brethren to
dwell together in unity!
—Psalm 133:1

It is good and pleasant when we fellowship and dwell together, when we practice shared love, receiving it from God and giving it to other people. When we are members of the Kingdom of God, that's where our citizenship lies. We become "peculiar people" (1 Peter 2:9 KJV) which means that we will be different from the people around us in our world. We do not have to be "of the world" to be in the world or to influence the world (John 17:14–18).

Jesus was different, yet He still went over to Matthew's house, the tax collector who was despised by many in the religious society (Matthew 9:9). He talked to sinners, and He spent time with people who didn't know God—but He still remained Jesus. We never have to compromise our values, but at the same time we should never become so separated from the world around us that we turn our backs on the needs of the people we see.

Did you know that Jesus commanded us to love those who are in the world and be kind to them? Colossians 4:5–6 says, "Be wise in the way you act toward those who are not believers, making good use of every opportunity you have. Your speech should always be pleasant and interesting, and you should know how to give the right answer to everyone" (GNT).

If you are saying to yourself, "It's me and Jesus together against the world," that's not actually the will of God for your life. Jesus has commanded us to have fellowship with other people, to "love one another" (John 13:34). There are four "one anothers" that He has asked us to live out in our relationships. Once we receive these four "one anothers" from Him, we can then turn around and give them to the people He places in our path.

Love One Another

> A new commandment I give to you, that you love one another; as I have loved you, that you also love one another. By this all will know that you are My disciples, if you have love for one another." Now, Jesus had just told His disciples that He was going to depart and that He wouldn't be with them for much longer. It is at that time in their relationship that He gave them this commandment.
> —*John 13:34–35*

Out of all of the things that Jesus could have told His disciples when He was about to leave their presence physically, what He commanded them to do was to love one another. Love was Jesus' greatest priority. In fact, it is the basis for all of the other "one anothers" that follow. Love is the one distinguishing mark of being a disciple of Jesus. He said, "By this [by love for one another] all will know that you are My disciples."

Consider that for a moment. How do other people know that you are a Christian? Is it because you can quote Scripture? Is it because you faithfully attend church every Sunday? Is it because you speak in tongues or you know how to lay your hands-on people and pray for them to be healed?

No. If we think that these things are what define us as Christians, we're missing the mark. Jesus made it very simple for us to understand. He said that if we love one another, that is how everyone will know that we are His disciples.

Love for one another is the one telltale sign that should make the world around us say, "That person must be a Christian!" Jesus identifies this love as different from any other love, because He calls it a new commandment. The Old Testament—truly, the entire Bible—is filled with the evidence of God's love. Even under the Old Covenant, God brought His people through the Red Sea (Exodus 14:21–22), and He provided manna for them in the desert (Exodus 16:4–5).

We can name situation after situation where God did something for His people. But in the New Testament we come to the point in the God–man relationship that God is dwelling with mankind *in the flesh* (John 1:14).

Jesus showed us the immense love that the Father God has for each and every one of us. And now He is telling us His greatest command: to love one another as He has loved us—with unconditional love.

Unconditional love is a love based on our commitment to another person, not based on what they do or do not do. If love were only based on emotion, none of us would still be here by now, because either God would have killed us all or we would have killed each other. Instead He acts toward us in a completely different way, loving us unconditionally, because of who He is and not how we behave. And Jesus doesn't ask—He *commands* us to love one another. If you claim today to follow the Lord Jesus Christ, then you must follow His commandment to love other people.

Encourage One Another

Therefore encourage one another and build each other up, just as in fact you are doing.
—1 Thessalonians 5:11 (NIV)

The second "one another" is to encourage one another. We will encourage one another if we love one another because we will want to help each other become the very best we can be. We can accomplish this in God's way by encouraging one another even in correction.

Have you ever been upset when you saw someone going down the wrong path because you didn't want to see them suffer the trouble that path would cause them? Even when you correct someone in your life, your motivation must be love (Ephesians 4:16). Your greatest concern must be for that other person to be restored and to grow in their relationship with God. If you have any other motivation than that, you are outside of the will of God.

If you are correcting someone with anger or self-righteousness rather than an attitude of encouragement in your heart, no matter how much you quote Scripture, you will still be in the wrong. Your attitude toward the other person and your internal motives are what God will consider when He judges your actions, and He tells us that we need to encourage one another.

If you must have a difficult conversation with someone to correct them or challenge them in their behavior, check your heart first. Ask the Lord to remove all judgment or bitterness and realize that if it were not for God's grace working in your own life, you could also be in the same situation. Correct the other person with that kind of love and heart motivation, and you will encourage them and motivate them to get back onto the right path.

In addition, encouragement goes a step beyond compassion. Some people believe that compassion is enough, that if they have compassion for the lost, the sick, and the weak, they are doing what God has asked them to do. Compassion will move you to pray for them and to hope that things get better for them, but encouragement means that you are taking a step toward someone and reaching into their life. You are not just praying for them from afar; you are calling them on the phone, going over to their house, taking their hand, and lifting them up, actively taking practical steps to help them out of their situation. When you are encouraging someone, you are extending God's love to them.

So be sure to give encouragement freely! We all need recognition for our accomplishments or we lose our motivation to continue. Even if someone seems to be doing well on the surface, or have it all together on the outside, that person may be on the verge of giving up on the inside. We never know what encouragement people really need. Few people make the need known quite as clearly as the little boy who said to his father, "Let's play darts. I'll throw the darts, and you say 'wonderful.'"[5]

Don't wait until tomorrow to encourage the people whom the Lord puts on your heart. If someone is on your mind, give them a call right away to encourage them. You can be His instrument of healing and love in a world filled with discouraged people. In this way, you will be showing forth God's love to those who really need it.

Forgive One Another

Therefore, as the elect of God, holy and beloved, put on tender mercies, kindness, humility, meekness, longsuffering; bearing with one another, and forgiving one another, if anyone has a complaint against another; even as Christ forgave you, so you also must do.
—Colossians 3:12–13

Forgiving one another is more than lip service, just like the other "one anothers" are. You may say, "I forgive you," but what about your heart? If you look deep inside, has anything really changed despite the words that are coming out of your mouth? In Ephesians 4:32, Paul told the Church, "And be kind to one another, tenderhearted, forgiving one another, *even as God in Christ forgave you."*

Now that was some forgiveness that God provided! On the cross, Jesus had all the sins of the world placed on His shoulders—all our past sin, all our present sin, and any sin that would ever be committed in the future (1 Peter 2:24). All of that was put on Him, yet He still forgave. How much more should we then forgive one another (Matthew 18:21–35)? By giving up the offense. By releasing the other person from the hurt that they have caused us. By not rehashing it in our thoughts and our conversations any more. If you have not been able to yet reach this level of forgiveness, ask God to help you achieve it. He stands ready to help; after all, His Son is the Master of Forgiveness.

Forgiveness is necessary, and we know it. The problem for us comes when we have to stop talking about it and start doing it. Not long before Marghanita Laski died in 1988, there was a moment of surprising candor in television. Laski was a secular humanist and a novelist, and in an interview shortly before her death, she said: "What I envy most about you Christians is your forgiveness. I have nobody to forgive me."[6] Sadly, she died that way, without knowing the forgiveness of others and likely the forgiveness of God.

If we are truly following Christ, then even though we as believers are no different from anyone else in the flesh, we are called to act differently in our forgiveness of other people—not to hold a grudge, to let the other person *completely* off the hook. What makes us different from the rest of the sinful, fallen world around us is our relationship with Jesus Christ. We are loved and forgiven by Christ, and He is the difference in our lives. That is what enables us to forgive other people and love them the way that He has loved us.

Serve One Another

For you, brethren, have been called to liberty; only do not use liberty as an opportunity for the flesh, but through love serve one another
—Galatians 5:13

Finally, we are called to serve one another. Let's choose to use our newly given liberty to love as God has loved us as an opportunity to serve other people. Why? Because all the laws of God are fulfilled in one word, in one command: To love—and thus, serve—your neighbor as yourself.

If we claim to be disciples of the Lord Jesus Christ, then we will be servants to other people because He was. Jesus said, "the Son of Man did not come to be served, but to serve" (Matthew 20:28). The Lord of the universe, the One who created you, the One who formed you in the womb, who fearfully and wonderfully made you, who blew the breath of life into you, He has served you. And now He asks that you be a servant to the people around you.

But the end of all things is at hand; therefore be serious and watchful in your prayers. And above all things have fervent love for one another, for "love will cover a

multitude of sins." Be hospitable to one another without grumbling. As each one has received a gift, minister it to one another, as good stewards of the manifold grace of God.
—1 Peter 4:7–10

The world in which we live teaches everyone to scramble to get to the top, that the highest leadership position is the best. We can chase so many things: money, glory, esteem, a higher position on the social and economic ladder. But Jesus washed the feet of His disciples, and He demonstrated respect and esteem for them in a greater way (John 13:1–17). He showed us the Kingdom way, in which the first will be last and the last will be first (Luke 13:30).

In the church, a person should be taught to strive to be the chief servant. We must serve each other voluntarily, out of love for one another and not to be seen and rewarded. Do the jobs that nobody else wants to do. Perform acts of love anonymously, with no chance of self-service or reward. Find an area within the church that needs your gifts, talents, and abilities, and offer to help. And do so with a spirit of humility and love, sharing the love that the Father has showered into your life.

When we love one another, encourage one another, forgive one another, and serve one another, we do so because of our Lord's example and by His power. The first step on this new road is to accept the Lord Jesus Christ and what He has done for you because without Him you will never be able to live a life of love. But with Him, you will be able to share all these things with the hurting people around you, allowing them to experience God's heart of love through your own hands and feet.

Chapter Four Questions

Question: Describe an occasion when someone encouraged you at a moment that made a big difference in your life. What are some practical ways that a believer can create a culture of encouragement in their home, church, workplace or school, and community (including online)?

_____

_____

_____

_____

_____

_____

_____

_____

_____

Question: What is the believer's motivation to forgive? Why is forgiveness so important?

_____

_____

_____

_____

_____

_____

_____

_____

_____

_____

Question: What is the attitude of a Christ-follower regarding service to one another?

_____

_____

_____

_____

_____

_____

_____

_____

_____

_____

Action: *Love, encourage, forgive, and serve one another.* Which one do you do well? Which one needs the most improvement? With an accountability partner, draw up a plan about how you will begin practicing that "one another" consistently in your life. Ask them to check back with you at one week, two weeks, one month, two months, and six months to see how you are progressing.

_____

_____

_____

_____

_____

_____

_____

_____

_____

_____

_____

_____

_____

Chapter Four Notes

_____

_____

_____

_____

_____

_____

_____

_____

_____

_____

_____

_____

_____

_____

_____

_____

_____

_____

_____

CHAPTER FIVE

Transformation

I beseech you therefore, brethren, by the mercies of God, that you present your bodies a living sacrifice, holy, acceptable to God, which is your reasonable service. And do not be conformed to this world, but be transformed by the renewing of your mind, that you may prove what is that good and acceptable and perfect will of God.
—Romans 12:1–2

You have a destiny! You have a destination, something God put before you that only you can accomplish, and you must begin to choose the pathways that will move you toward that destination. God loves you too much to leave you the way you are. He wants to transform you into something else, someone more like Himself.

You may already be familiar with these first verses of Romans 12. Presenting your body as a living sacrifice, following through with what God has asked you to do in this world—is really the least that you can do, considering everything that God has done for you. That is, truly, your "reasonable service."

But then the Scriptures take it a step further. As Paul writes, "And do not be conformed to this world, but be transformed by the renewing of your mind, that you may prove what is that good and acceptable and perfect will of God" (Romans 12:2). God doesn't want you just to try to fulfill His permissible will in your life, the things that He would allow you to do. No, we are talking about the perfect will of God. Get the "permissible" mindset out of your head. Even if you have done something a certain way for years, that does not mean it is the best way.

What does God really want for your life? The Bible tells us very clearly: "what is good and acceptable and perfect" (Romans 12:2) His goals for us are only for our good! Unlike our enemy, the devil, God wants good, acceptable, and perfect things for us.

Jesus was the One who said, "The thief does not come except to steal, and to kill, and to destroy. I have come that they may have life, and that they may have it more abundantly" (John 10:10). God came and wrapped Himself in a body of human flesh. He died on a bloody cross and was dead for three days. Then Christ rose again on the third day with all power and is now seated at the right hand of the Father. He did all this so that you might have life more abundantly.

He came not just so you would have life, but so you would have it more abundantly—more joy, more peace, more *love*—than you could ever imagine.

In fact, the reason for your very existence is to understand the greatest Force in the universe, the love of God, and to be renewed and transformed by that love so that you might have a relationship with the Lord. Then you are to share that same grace, mercy, and love that He gives you with the undeserving. He wants you to share it not just with people who seem worthy to you, but with those who don't deserve it.

I have a secret for you: *you* didn't deserve it! You didn't deserve the extravagance that God has poured out upon you. You didn't deserve the grace that He gave you. You didn't deserve the mercy that endures forever, that is new every morning. None of us deserve it, but He offers it to us anyway. Now it is up to you and me to share that same extravagance with others, to be so transformed by God's love and overflowing with it that we can't wait to share it with the world.

Growing Up in Christ

God's Word tells us to be transformed by the renewing of our minds (Romans 12:2). In the realm of nature, we can see that a caterpillar transforms itself from what is essentially a glorified earthbound worm into a beautiful butterfly. It moves from an immature state into mature adulthood. That is what a metamorphosis is: moving from an immature, childlike state into that of a fully-grown adult (1 Corinthians 13:11). God intends for His people to go through a process of maturation.

You can't give a little child the keys to the car. Even when children reach the age where they can start to do some things for themselves, you still need to tell them exactly what to do. With a small child, you don't just say, "I want you to go upstairs and take a bath." You can't leave it at that. You have to say, "I want you to go upstairs and take your clothes off. I want you to turn the water on. Then get some soap and put it in the tub. But before you do that, put the stopper in the drain so the water doesn't just run out. When the water gets up to a certain level, turn it off. Get into the bathtub, get a washcloth with some soap, and then wash it across your body."

Those are instructions for a little child, but God wants to take us to the point where He can say, "Take a bath," and we know what to do. We don't have to ask Him about every detail, because we know Him, and we have listened to His teachings. Seek His guidance about the questions you have in your life, but also trust that His Holy Spirit will guide you from the inside, that He will grow you up as a Christian. He wants you to be transformed, to undergo the metamorphosis from a caterpillar into a beautiful butterfly.

Don't Conform; Transform!

There is an important difference between the words "conform" and "transform" in Romans 12:2. Paul essentially told us, "Don't let the world *conform* you." If we are not careful, the world will conform us from the outside in. It moves upon us and changes the way we think, our perspective. You see certain things take place in the world: political scandals, school shootings, racial injustice, human trafficking, poverty, drug abuse, disease. When you see all these things out in the world, they begin to conform you and your worldview, your way of thinking. You begin to be changed.

Yes, your environment will shape you, but God is

saying, "That's not what I want to see happening in your life. I know that you're extraordinary. You belong to Me. I want to come inside you and change you, starting with your heart and your mind. I want to transform you from the inside out!"

Consider what happened to Jesus on the Mount of Transfiguration. He was transformed from the inside out, and His disciples were allowed to see what a real spiritual being looked like (Matthew 17:1–13). Here's news for you: You are the same type of spiritual being as Jesus was on that mountain. If you have given your life to Christ and He has truly changed you, then you are the same spiritual being that Jesus was. There is something important that God has placed inside of you, something that He wants you to share with the world.

The transformation that is taking place in us needs to come out and bless those around us in our world, but we first have to allow God to have His way on the inside of us. Too often we try to do it on our own. We let what other people say about us conform us, mold us, and shape who we are. We get offended by people, and we react to what they do.

Other people may say to us, "You can't accomplish anything in this life. You're no good. You're not smart enough. You don't have the right degree to do what you are planning to do." There will always be other people in this world who will seek to bring you down, and if you allow them to do so, you are being conformed.

Listen instead to what God is telling you: "You are the head and not the tail! I made you to be above and never again be beneath. You're blessed in the city. You are blessed in the field. You are blessed when you go out and when you come in" (Deuteronomy 28:3–6, 13). When are we going to start believing what God says about us and what He has transformed us into?

The Bible tells us, "Therefore, if anyone is in Christ, he is a new creation; old things have passed away; behold, all things have become new" (2 Corinthians 5:17). What old things is God referring to in this verse? The time of being offended and offending others has passed away. Your old attitude of being self-centered, unkind, and ashamed has passed away. In His Word, God invites us to "behold, all things have become new!" (2 Corinthians 5:17). God's mercies are new every morning (Lamentations 3:23). We never have to be stuck in who we used to be. It is a new day!

When a caterpillar transforms into a butterfly, the process is fascinating. A caterpillar will eat and eat and eat—until suddenly one day it stops. After that, it starts spinning its cocoon. It covers itself with the cocoon material, and inside of it, the caterpillar breaks itself down into almost a liquid-like form. Then it begins to digest itself. The caterpillar has to kill off everything from its previous life that it will not need when it becomes a butterfly. A few cells do remain, and those cells are what begin to develop into the new body.

Similarly, when God transforms you from the inside out, there are some things that you will need to break down. There are some things on the inside of you that will need to be killed off.

What kinds of things will you not need when you reach your final transformation into a fully mature Christian?

Certainly, you need to let some self-serving, worldly attitudes and negative ways of thinking die. You need to rid yourself of anything that is not part of God's good and perfect will (Romans 12:2), because He wants to shape you into something other than what you are right now, something greater. He wants to do it, but we also have to allow Him to do it.

First Corinthians 15:53 states: "For this corruptible must put on incorruption, and this mortal must put on immortality." The Good News Translation (GNT) puts it this way: "For what is mortal must be changed into what is immortal; what will die must be changed into what cannot die."

When you read this verse in its context, you see that a day is coming when the Lord Jesus will return, and we will all be changed in the twinkling of an eye (1 Corinthians 15:52 NIV). On that day, we will become spirit forms. We will shed our bodies of flesh and bone, and our true selves will shine forth as pure gold. You may be praying this prayer, "Please be patient with me. God is not through with me yet," but you could also add on the phrase: "because when He is finished with me, I shall come forth as pure gold."

The moment you gave your life to the Lord and you made Jesus the Lord and King of your heart, when you confessed that He was killed, was buried, and was raised on the third day, and you believed it in your heart—at that very moment, all the old things in your life passed away, and a new Spirit entered your heart. The breath of God came in and awakened your understanding. It is almost as if God yelled to you in the spirit, "Wake up! I am making you new!" When He makes you new, you will come forth as an eternal being. That eternal being is inside of you right now; it's the real you, just waiting for mortality to put on immortality.

No matter what happens, God is still in control. Many Christians get saved and say, "Lord, I will give my life to You." They begin to be discipled, and great things begin to happen. They give the offering in faith, and they are amazed at how God supplies their needs. But eventually, inevitably, something bad will happen. Somebody might say unkind things about them, or a situation might not work out the way that they thought it should, and they become discouraged. Maybe they question their faith.

They begin to listen to others, and they become conformed. They lose their focus on God and choose a different path, apart from His will. How many of us have a call on our lives, have books in us that are unwritten, have great things in us that God has already placed there, but because other people have told us who we are and what we cannot do, we begin to act in lesser ways than our true callings?

That is not what God wants for our lives. All of us need to undergo such a complete change that we allow God to take over our entire world. We give Him our hearts and our minds. We allow Him to be the one to shape our thoughts, our perspectives, and our desires. We cannot fix ourselves. Only He can transform us into His image, into the men and women He wants us to be, those who are His instruments of change in this world.

And what will be the result of that transformation? Keep in mind the following goals:

Goals of Transformation

The first goal of transformation is simply to become like Christ. One of the best ways to do that is to grab your Bible. Before you do anything, go to the Word of God. Seek His will and His truth. Then bow your head and pray, because when you do that, God will put you back on the correct path.

The second goal of transformation is to take it to the next level and live like Christ. How would He treat others? The Bible tells us to treat others in the way that we would want to be treated (Matthew 7:12). We are to love and forgive and serve as Jesus did. This tends to be difficult for us to do, because many people get on our nerves.

But to that I can imagine Christ saying, "Really? You don't say. Well, people got on My nerves, too, but I still went to the cross. I was in the Garden of Gethsemane, sweating blood for people who would ultimately turn their backs on Me, for people who would tell lies about Me and spit on Me, for people who would betray Me (Luke 22:44). I chose to forgive. If I forgive people and yet they will not move on to forgive others, then what have I done all of this for?"

Jesus didn't do everything that He did just because of what you would do for Him. No, He did it because of who He is, for His own glory, and because He has set His love upon you. But this love He gives you isn't meant to stop with you. You need to extend it to others. That's the tough part, where the rubber meets the road.

If you want to rise above your circumstances, try doing things the Kingdom way. Try forgiving people. Try praying for your enemies and those who persecute you. Yes, you should be good to the people who are nice to you, but you also need to show kindness towards those who are unkind to you and try to take advantage of you.

The books of Matthew and Luke encourage us in this; they tell us: "Judge not, that you be not judged" (Matthew 7:1 ESV). I don't know about you, but I do not want God's judgment raining down upon my head for all of the times I've messed up and made the wrong choices. I would much rather let other people off the hook!

Give, and it will be given to you: good measure, pressed down, shaken together, and running over will be put into your bosom. For with the same measure that you use, it will be measured back to you.
—*Luke 6:38*

God's blessings are always beneficial to us in the end. He always gives us over and above what we give to Him. If I live my life-giving judgement to others, I certainly do not want to receive His judgment "in good measure, pressed down, shaken together, and running over." I would much rather have His forgiveness poured out on me in such a way! Stop judging. Just don't do it, because the way in which you judge is the way that you yourself are going to be judged.

Be transformed! Be set free! Allow your chains to be broken, for God wants to break every chain. You don't have to be caught up in your old self anymore. You can receive the gift of eternal life. You can receive peace with God. You can have access to the grace of God and experience His guidance and favor in every area of your life.

The greatest force in the universe has set itself in favor of you. God Himself has set His perfect love upon you. It is an unconditional, personal, life-giving, and life-changing love—and it has been given to you for a reason. You can walk in God's grace every day of your life, but He wants you to share that grace with everyone around you. You will be blessed in the city and in the country, because there are other people in the city and in the country who also need the blessing of the Lord.

Paul gave us the key when he said, "Renew your mind!" (Romans 12:2). The process of transformation continues as we renew our minds, and this is made possible when we set our minds on what He has called us to do: to be a force for His good in the world around us.

Feed Your Mind

Sometimes you can't change your circumstances, especially when other people are involved. For instance, you can't always go out and just make your car work. You can lay hands on it, but you may not be able to fix it on your own. You may not have a quick fix or a solution for everything that goes on around you. That is not in your own strength, but here's where it starts: What you *can* do is set your mind on things above, according to Colossians 3:2, "Set your mind on things above, not on things on the earth." Quit dwelling on the petty stuff and consider an eternal perspective.

Think about taking off corruption and putting on

incorruption. Think about taking off mortality and putting on immortality. Set your mind on the things of the Spirit. Become preoccupied with demonstrating the fruit of the Spirit in your life: "But the fruit of the Spirit is love, joy, peace, longsuffering, kindness, goodness, faithfulness, gentleness, self-control. Against such there is no law" (Galatians 5:22–23).

You can do it! More importantly, God can do it through you. His transformative work is the only thing that will make a true, lasting difference in your life, the only way this can be accomplished. Feed your mind with the Word of God. Stop worrying about what's going on with the Kardashians or the latest plot twist on your favorite crime drama. Believe me, I have to watch myself with this, too. We get caught up in the latest gossip, office politics, entertainment news, and technology. We feed our minds with so many meaningless, distracting things.

Instead, try feeding your mind with the Word of God and see the difference it will make in your life. Feed on the Word. Don't just read it. Meditate on it (Psalm 1:2). Savor it. Dwell on it. Take the half hour when you would sit down and watch a TV show and instead read the Bible. Think about what you are reading. Ask the Lord to speak to you through His Word. Listen, concentrate, focus. Feed your mind with the Word of God because that is how your mind will be renewed. That is how you are going to grow as a follower of Christ and become ever more like Him.

When Jesus took a few of His followers up on the Mount of Transfiguration, He first talked to the Father, and then He was changed (Matthew 17:1–13). He heard the words of His heavenly Father, and then He allowed those disciples to see the moment of His life when He experienced the change that the Father had for Him.

Jesus shared with His twelve disciples the most intimate moments of His life. He was vulnerable with them. Be the same way with the people whom you disciple. You only have to be one step ahead. You don't have to be a theologian to disciple another person. Just keep following the Lord as they follow you; it's that simple.

This is how you will grow spiritually and how you will help to bring people into the Kingdom of God, by discipling. You have been called to be transformed into the image of Christ (2 Corinthians 3:18). You have all the motivation that you need to be transformed. You have the opportunity to start anew, you have the washing with the water of the Word, and you have the regeneration.

God wants to give you a complete makeover. The only question left for you is whether you will allow Him to do it or you will remain in the status quo. Are you going to allow God to transform you, starting with your mind, and change the way you think about yourself and your life and the way you see and treat other people?

I don't know about you, but I've been in church just about all my life, and if a church service is all there is— just attending, singing some songs, and listening to somebody talk at me from a pulpit once a week—then I'm over it. I've done it, seriously, and I don't need to do it again. I might go occasionally just to be entertained, but other than that, I don't want to be a part of a church like that. I could join another club to do that.

I want to be a part of something real, something meaningful, something that lasts. I want God to move in the core of my being. I want to experience His extravagant love and His eternal blessings overflowing in my life. And I want to give that powerful, soul-awakening, mind-altering love to the people He places in my path. Won't you join me? Together, with Him, we can change the world.

Chapter Five Questions

Question: Would people who know you well say that your life is best described as *conformed* to the world or *transformed* by God? In what areas are you most tempted to conform to the world and its values? In what areas has your life been transformed by a renewed mind?

_____

_____

_____

_____

_____

_____

_____

_____

Question: What is the difference between God instructing you as one would direct a small child, on the one hand, and the Holy Spirit guiding you as a grown up, on the other? How does one move into this maturity in Christ?

_____

_____

_____

_____

_____

_____

_____

_____

_____

_____

Question: What are the goals of a transformed life? What does a transformed life look like on a day-to-day basis? How do you need to feed your mind in order to see your life transformed?

_____

_____

_____

_____

_____

_____

_____

_____

_____

_____

_____

_____

Action: Look at the "food" you are giving your mind. Write out a list of everything that influences you—specific kinds of music, friends, books, television, social media, etc., that have your attention and loyalty. Next to each one write a C for conforming or a T for transforming. For those influences that are not helping to renew your mind in Christ, write a replacement that can help further you in your Christian growth and maturity.

_____

_____

_____

_____

_____

_____

_____

_____

Chapter Five Notes

_____

_____

_____

_____

_____

_____

_____

_____

_____

_____

_____

_____

_____

_____

_____

_____

_____

_____

_____

_____

CONCLUSION

The Extravagant Love of God

See what great love the Father has lavished on us, that we should be called children of God!
—1 John 3:1 (NIV)

How much love the Father has bestowed upon His children! And the more we receive from Him, the more He asks us to share. God's love is plentiful enough to go around. He has filled you up to overflowing with His goodness, His love, His kindness, and His generosity, and He wants you to spread these things to a hurting world. It will not diminish you to share His gifts with other people. It will open your heart to receive even more!

God's Spirit on the inside of you will guide you as you open yourself to Him. He will prompt you to notice the one who is in need: the frazzled single mother at McDonald's who could use a cup of coffee, the person scowling in the car next to you at the stoplight who needs a warm smile and a wave, the homeless man on the corner who could use a financial hand and a warm meal.

You have been blessed to be a blessing (Genesis 12:2). Rid yourself of selfishness. Get out of your comfort zone. Look at the world around you with God's eyes and a fresh perspective. And then take the step to reach out. You will begin a grand adventure of partnering with the Lord to reach the world through His lavish, extravagant love.

REFERENCES

Notes

1. "Professional Listener Finds People Will Pay to Be Heard." *Vernon Daily Record*. August 15, 1975. p. 3.
2. Petersen, J. Allan. *The Myth of the Greener Grass*. Tyndale House, 1983. In Craig Bryan Larson, *750 Illustrations for Preachers, Teachers, and Writers* (Baker Books, 2007), p. 319.
3. Sanford, David. "God's Definition of Love." *CBN.* http://www1.cbn.com/inspirational teaching/gods-definition-of-love.
4. Maestas, Jose Griego, and Rudolfo Anaya. "The Boy and His Grandfather." *Cuentos: Tales from the Hispanic Southwest*. Museum of New Mexico Press, 1980. In "Grandpa's Table, " *Moral Stories*. https://www.moralstories.org/grandpas-table.
5. "Let's Play Darts!" *Bible.org*. From *Bits & Pieces* (December 9, 1993), p. 24. https://bible.org/illustration/let's-play-darts.
6. "A Humanist's Lament." *Preaching Today*. November 1997. https://www.preachingtoday.com/illustrations/1997/november/915.html.

About the Author

Michael Carter and his wife Detra are the senior pastors at The Life Church in Bloomington, Indiana. Michael is a graduate of Indiana Wesleyan University in Business Science and Religious Studies. He and his wife pioneered and pastored Abundant Life Family Worship Center in Indianapolis, Indiana, for three years before returning home to become senior pastors of The Life Church. They served as worship leaders at The Life Church for seven years and as elders for three years. Michael has spoken to congregations around the world, including the Philippines, Romania, and Fiji. He and Detra have five children—four girls and one boy.

About Sermon To Book

SermonToBook.com began with a simple belief: that sermons should be touching lives, *not* collecting dust. That's why we turn sermons into high-quality books that are accessible to people all over the globe.

Turning your sermon series into a book exposes more people to God's Word, better equips you for counseling, accelerates future sermon prep, adds credibility to your ministry, and even helps make ends meet during tight times.

John 21:25 tells us that the world itself couldn't contain the books that would be written about the work of Jesus Christ. Our mission is to try anyway. Because in heaven, there will no longer be a need for sermons or books. Our time is now.

If God so leads you, we'd love to work with you on your sermon or sermon series.

Visit www.sermontobook.com to learn more.

www.ingramcontent.com/pod-product-compliance
Lightning Source LLC
LaVergne TN
LVHW052034080426
835513LV00018B/2319